Ash in the Attic

Chris Powling
Illustrated by Alan Marks

Rigby
A Harcourt Achieve Imprint

www.Rigby.com
1-800-531-5015

Asha loved Grandpa's attic.

It wasn't just big and dusty and full of stuff from the olden days. Most attics are like that. Grandpa's attic was special because of the stories Grandpa told there.

Once, while she was exploring, Asha found an old school bag. Grandpa's eyes lit up when he saw it.

"Now that reminds me of a story," he said. And he told Asha about the pet rat he took to school one day.

Another time, it was a medal.

"This story is scary," he warned her. "Also, a bit sad . . ." Grandpa told her about a friend of his who was hurt in the war.

Asha listened to every word.

Best of all, though, was the pile of baby clothes.

"Your mom wore these, Asha," Grandpa grinned. "I could tell you a story or two about her . . . once she threw all my tools in the pond to see how deep it was!"

Asha laughed and laughed.

By now, she couldn't wait for her next visit to the attic. What would she find when she got there? And what story would it jog in Grandpa's memory?

Only one thing bothered her.

"Grandpa?" she asked quietly. "Do you think . . ."

"Yes, Asha?"

"Do you think you'll ever . . ."

"Go on, my dear."

"Well . . . do you think you'll ever tell a story about me? Here, in the attic, I mean?"

"Here?" asked Grandpa with his eyebrows raised. "In the attic?"

Asha nodded.

Grandpa scratched his head.

"I'm bound to eventually," he said.
"But you may have to be patient,
Asha. After all, everything in this
big, dusty attic comes from the olden
days . . . there's nothing olden
day-ish about you!"

Poor Asha. She didn't want to be patient. She wanted to be in one of Grandpa's stories now.

Then, she had an idea. Suppose she hid Owen, her stuffed owl, in Grandpa's attic? And suppose she pretended to find it in some far corner? Grandpa would have to tell an Asha-story then, wouldn't he?

So, while Grandpa was snoozing
out in the sun, Asha crept back into
the house.

She tiptoed up and up the stairs, right to the top of the house.

"Here's the door to the attic, Owen," she said. "Let's shut it tight so Grandpa won't see where I'm hiding you."

Now, for the first time ever, Asha had the attic all to herself.

Slowly, she turned around. It had never looked so big or so dusty or so full of stuff from the olden days.

It had never looked so lonely, either. Asha felt a shiver along her spine.

"I can't leave you here, Owen," she whispered. "I'm not sure I can stay here myself."

She turned to leave and found the door was stuck. Asha tugged it and jiggled it and kicked it as hard as she could. She shouted, too, at the top of her voice.

But the door stayed stuck.

What could Asha do?

"Grandpa can't hear us, Owen," she said. "These old floor boards are so thick. We must be patient until he realizes where we are. Don't worry. We'll share some stories to pass the time."

Luckily, Asha knew lots of stories. She settled down to tell them on Grandpa's old sofa under the skylight.

First came the schoolbag story. Then the stories about the baby clothes. After this, Asha began the story of the medal.

"It's scary, Owen," she warned. "Also, a bit sad . . ."

Suddenly, Asha heard a strange noise. It was a sneaky, creaky, skylight-opening noise.

A dark figure loomed overhead. Was a burglar breaking in?

Asha shrank back in alarm.

"Don't be frightened, Owen," she gasped. "It's only . . . it's only . . .

GRANDPA!"

He'd come to rescue Asha, of
course. Now that he was inside the
attic, he soon loosened the door.

Afterward, he sat on the sofa with Asha and Owen.

"What a brave pair you are," he said. "Plenty of people would have panicked, you know. Would you like to hear my new story? It's called ASHA IN THE ATTIC."

"Can I tell it, Grandpa?" Asha
giggled. Grandpa let her, of course.
"Asha loved Grandpa's attic . . ."